THE
EXOTIC
COOKBOOK

THE
EXOTIC
COOKBOOK

Recipes compiled by
Delroy Neita

Introduction by
Ivor Osbourne

Illustrations by
Robin Collingwood

ACKNOWLEDGEMENTS

The Publisher and Authors wish to express thanks to all who have helped to make this book possible and special thanks to:

Charlene Mertens, Desmond Johnson (editorial)
Robin Collingwood (illustrations)
Terry Howe (final art)

First published in paperback 1990 by
Macdonald Optima, a division of
Macdonald & Co. (Publishers) Ltd.

A member of Maxwell Macmillan Pergamon Publishing Corporation

British Library Cataloguing in Publication Data
NEITA, D.A.
The Exotic Low Calorie Cookbook
1. Food: West Indian Dishes. Recipes
1 Title 641.5'635
ISBN 0-356-18149-9

Macdonald & Co. (Publishers) Ltd.
Orbit House
1 New Fetter Lane
London EC4A 1AR

Printed in Great Britain by
Richard Clay Ltd, Bungay, Suffolk

THE
EXOTIC
COOKBOOK

INTRODUCTION

The 'Indies', the mythical islands of spice, once the goal of many an adventurer and the subject of many a dream are now only but a few hours away. The audience can no longer be held with tales of such journeys or sojourns.

In the last decade alone travel and trade between east and west, the old world and the new has increased to hitherto almost unimaginable proportions. And growing alongside this increasing flux we are seeing an ever widening range of new produce and products appearing on the shelves at the local grocery store.

At the corner shop, the local grocer is selling fresh Peruvian mangoes and next to this, Kiwi fruit and Israeli avocados.

In the street markets the erstwhile yam is no longer a total stranger. And although sometimes eyed, as with many of its tropical companions, only from a distance with a mixture of curiosity and foreboding, its presence on the shelves seems to have taken on a kind of permanency.

What seems certain is that once the wary shopper falls to the temptation of first purchase, or first taste, he becomes converted, and there is little backsliding.

Day-to-day eating habits, in so far as the range of foods eaten and the method of preparation, have been undergoing rapid transformation over the last decade.

In the inner cities, eating out is now almost a way of saying that one is going out to experiment with new foods. In fact, the traditional restaurant is now a rarity on the high streets in most of the world's capital cities, the centres of fashion, culture and 'taste'. Indeed in London it is easier to eat Japanese than to eat traditional English fare; foreign restaurants, or English restaurants serving foreign food of one description or another, simply clutter the nightlife areas.

The days of 'meat and two veg' are rapidly becoming a thing of the past.

And along with this change of eating habits has come an increasing consciousness of how what we eat affects our health and well being.

Evolving from this is a new and more international cuisine, a more healthy cuisine, selecting and mixing food from the regions of the world in the preparation of daily meals.

This book presents a mere sample of what delights await the most timid among us, those who can brave to select only the vegetable least alien in appearance from the shelf.

Drawing on his experience in the preparation of both tropical and temperate zone foods Delroy Neita provides a skilful guide to the blending of these 'exotic' foods into the fare of the traditional 'roast beef dinner', the blend of the exotic and the ordinary, the tropical and the temperate.

Again however, as with other books in this series, the recipes as presented are not intended to serve as a book of rules, or as a limit to experimentation. The intention is to provide you with background information, through examples, on flavours and methods of preparation, to remove the veil of strangeness which surrounds some of these new additions to our daily diet.

Each recipe adheres to the concept of healthy eating for the omnivore and is calorie counted by serving portion.

Eat for your health.

Ivor Osbourne, 1989

CONTENTS

BEVERAGES

Rum Punch

Sorrel Wine

Guinness Cocktail

Pineapple Juice Cocktail

Carrot Juice Cocktail

Mango Punch

Rum Punch

Ingredients

$^1/_4$ cup lime juice, $^1/_2$ cup brown sugar
1 cup cold water, 1 cup rum
nutmeg (grated)

Method

Dissolve sugar in water then add rum and lime juice.
Blend and chill.

Serving

Serve with crushed ice, adding a pinch of nutmeg to each glass.

Serves 4

Calories: 80 per portion

Sorrel Wine

Ingredients

$1/4$ lb dried sorrel, $1/4$ teaspoon cinnamon spice
orange peel (dried), $1/2$ teaspoon green ginger
2 lb brown sugar, 2 whole cloves
4 pints boiling water
8 tablespoons rum

Method

Place dried sorrel, orange peel, cinnamon and cloves into a bowl and pour the boiling water over. Allow to cool then cover and leave the mixture to stand in a cool place for 2 days.

Strain to remove the residues then add sugar, rum and powdered spices. Allow to stand for a further 3 days.

Serving

Serve chilled, with crushed ice.

Serves 12

Calories: 125 per portion

Guinness Cocktail

Ingredients

1 pint Guinness Stout, 4 tablespoons honey
4 tablespoons brown sugar, 1 pint soya milk
nutmeg (powdered/grated)

Method

Blend the ingredients together for 2-3 minutes then pour into
serving glasses.

Serving

Best served with crushed ice.

Serves 4

Calories: 96 per portion

Pineapple Juice Cocktail

Ingredients

6 tablespoons honey
$^1/_2$ pint evaporated milk
1 pint pineapple juice
nutmeg, vanilla essence

Method

Blend all the ingredients together for 2-3 minutes, chill then pour into individual glasses.

Serving

Best served with crushed ice.

Serves 6

Calories: 150 per portion

Hints: Soya milk can be used as a substitute for evaporated milk.

Carrot Juice Cocktail

Ingredients

1 lb fresh carrots
4 oz brown sugar
3 tablespoons brandy
1 pint soya milk
nutmeg

Method

Blend/liquidise carrots to a puree then add milk, brandy, sugar and nutmeg. Blend for a further 2-3 minutes. Then chill and pour into serving glasses.

Serving

Best served with crushed ice.

Serves 6

Calories: 175 per portion

Hints: A slice of fresh orange can be added to each glass when serving.

Mango Punch

Ingredients

4 ripe medium-sized mangoes
lime juice (1 lime), $1^1/_2$ pints cold water
honey

Method

Remove skins from the mangoes; cut away the flesh from the stone and place this in a blender with the water, lime juice and honey to taste.

Blend the mixture for 2-3 minutes. Chill.

Serving

Serve well chilled.

Serves 4

Calories: 105 per portion

SNACKS AND APPETISERS

Caribbean Vegetable Omelette

Stuffed Avocado

Stuffed Green Peppers

Breadfruit Fritters

Sweetcorn Fritters

Baked Plantains

Baked Bananas

Caribbean Vegetable Omelette

Ingredients

6 green bananas
1 medium sized onion
$^1/_2$ pint (275 ml) water
2 tablespoons wholemeal flour
$^1/_2$ teaspoon grated nutmeg
4 tablespoons vegetable oil

Method

Peel and finely chop the onion. Slice the ends of each banana, cut
it in half, crossways, then using a sharp knife slit through the skin
to the flesh along the length of each half. Prise away the skins
with your fingers. Place the flesh of the bananas in a blender and
puree adding a little water at a time until you have a smooth
puree. Pour into a bowl, add the chopped onion then gradually
stir in the flour and nutmeg.

Bring the oil to heat in a frying pan and pour in the mixture, fry
gently on both sides to a golden brown.

Serving

Divide into individual portions and serve with a salad.

Serves 6

Calories: 125 per portion

Stuffed Avocado

Ingredients

1 lb (450 g) tomatoes
¼ pint (150 ml) yogurt
3 slices peeled root ginger
freshly ground black pepper
lime juice (1 lime)
2 large avocados

Method

Blanch and peel the tomatoes, cut them into halves and wash them in a colander under a stream of cold water to remove the seeds. Place tomatoes into a blender, add yogurt, lime juice and black pepper to taste, then blend until smooth.

Chop the slices of ginger finely and stir into the mixture.

Halve the avocados and remove the stones.

Serving

Heap the mixture into the centre of the avocado halves then garnish with a sprinkling of paprika.

Serves 4

Calories: 270 per portion

Stuffed Green Peppers

Ingredients

2 medium-sized green peppers
20 oz (550 g) ackees, 2 medium-sized tomatoes
2 spring onions, freshly ground black pepper

Method

Blanch, peel and chop the tomatoes. Slice the spring onions into small lengths.

Place ackees in a saucepan with the tomatoes and spring onions and allow to simmer under a gentle heat for approximately 20 minutes. Allow to cool.

Halve the peppers lengthways and remove the seeds and pith. Place these halves in a saucepan, cover with water. Bring to boil and then allow to simmer for 15 minutes. Allow to cool then remove the skin from the peppers.

Serving

Simply heap the ackee/tomato mix into the pepper halves, one half per serving and garnish with a sprinkling of paprika.

Serves 4

Calories: 208 per portion

Hints: Best served cold

Breadfruit Fritters

Ingredients

$\frac{1}{2}$ breadfruit, 1 clove garlic
2 tablespoons soya milk, 3 oz (85 g) wholemeal flour
$\frac{1}{4}$ tablespoon paprika, fresh ground black pepper
vegetable oil, 1 egg

Method

Cut the breadfruit into 4 wedges, remove and discard the skin and heart from each wedge with a sharp knife. Place the breadfruit in a saucepan containing a pint of water, salted to taste, bring to boil and cook until tender (about 30 minutes) on low heat. Pour away the water and leave the breadfruit to cool.

Strip and chop the garlic finely and add this to the soya milk, egg, flour, paprika and pepper to taste in a bowl. Mix these ingredients to a smooth paste.

Dip each breadfruit segment into the paste then fry in the vegetable oil at low heat, frying both sides until golden brown.

Serving

Serve with a small salad garnish

Serves 4

Calories: 210 per portion

Sweetcorn Fritters

Ingredients

3 oz wholemeal flour
1 medium sized onion
8 oz (225 g) sweetcorn (off the cob)
1 clove garlic, 1 egg
4 tablespoons soya milk
vegetable oil for frying

Method

Cook the sweetcorn in a pint of water until tender (15 minutes).
Drain and allow to cool.

Peel and finely chop the onion and garlic and add these,
along with the wholemeal flour, black pepper (to taste) and egg to
the sweetcorn in a bowl. Mix together with a wooden spoon to a
stiff paste.

Heat the oil in a saucepan and add the sweetcorn mix in separate,
tablespoon sized drops, frying each side on low heat until golden
brown.

Serving

Serve with a garnish of salad.

Serves 4

Calories: 80 per portion

Baked Bananas

Ingredients

4 large ripe bananas
2 oz (55 g) vegetable oil
2 tablespoons honey, 4 tablespoons lime juice
$1/4$ tablespoon pimento berries

Method

Peel the bananas and slice into two, lengthways and lay the halves side by side in a greased (using the oil) oven tray or heatproof dish.

Mix the honey and lime juice and pour the mixture over the banana slices.

Crush the pimento berries and sprinkle over the bananas then bake in a pre-heated oven Gas Mark 4 (200°C) for 20 minutes.

Serving

Serve hot.

Serves 4

Calories: 205 per portion

Hints: This dish also makes an excellent dessert served with ice cream or fresh cream.

Baked Plantains

Ingredients

4 large ripe plantains
2 oz vegetable oil
2 tablespoons honey
4 tablespoons orange juice
$1/4$ teaspoon ground nutmeg

Method

Peel and slice each plantain into two halves, lengthways, and lay halves side by side in a baking tray lined with foil (use oil to grease foil).

Mix the honey, orange juice and nutmeg and pour this mixture over the plantain slices.

Bake at Gas Mark 4 (200°C) for 25 minutes.

Serving

Serve hot.

Serves 6

Calories: 215 per portion

Hints: Although related to the banana, the plantain has a distinctly different taste, and unlike the banana is not usually eaten uncooked.

SOUPS

Ackee and Cho Cho Soup

Callaloo and Green Banana Soup

Sweetcorn and Pumpkin Soup

Breadfruit and Ackee Soup

Caribbean Vegetable Soup

Ackee and Cho Cho Soup

Ingredients

1 tin of ackees (20 oz), 1 cho cho
1 pint (55 ml) chicken stock
2 tomatoes ($^1/_2$ lb), 2 spring onions
ground black pepper

Method

Peel the cho cho, cut into six wedges. Cut away and discard the
heart (fibrous central portion) from the wedges, then dice into
1 inch thick cubes. Blanch and peel the tomatoes and roughly
chop the spring onions. Drain away the brine and empty the tin of
ackees into a large saucepan. Add the chicken stock. Add the
diced cho cho, tomatoes, spring onions and black pepper to the
saucepan and bring to the boil. Cover and simmer the soup on a
gentle heat for 30 minutes. Allow to cool then liquidise in a
blender.

Serving

Return to the saucepan and reheat before serving. Serve each
portion with a sprinkling of chilli powder.

Serves 4

Calories: 214 per portion

Note: Ackees are part of the national dish of Jamaica and are
rarely available fresh outside that island. They are however readily
available canned in brine.

Callaloo and Green Banana Soup

Ingredients

4 large green bananas (1 lb)
2 spring onions, 2 cloves garlic
1 pint (550 ml) chicken stock, 2 sprigs of thyme
1 green sweet pepper, ground black pepper
2 lb callaloo

Method

Remove all the leaves from the callaloo stem, wash and drain then roughly chop. Cut each banana into 4 wedges by cutting across and then along the length of each half. Halve the green pepper, discard the seeds, then dice into 1 inch thick pieces. Finely chop the spring onions and garlic.

Place these vegetables into a large saucepan. Add the chicken stock, cloves, thyme and ground black pepper. Bring the soup to the boil and simmer for 20-25 minutes. Remove the banana quarters, peel and discard the skin then return them to the soup. Liquidise in a blender then serve.

Serving

Add a little natural yogurt (3-4 tablespoons) to each portion and stir.

Serves 4-6

Calories: 198 per portion

Note: Spinach can be used as a substitute for callaloo.

Sweetcorn and Pumpkin Soup

Ingredients

$^1/_2$ lb sweetcorn (kernels)
2 pints (1100 ml) chicken stock
1 lb (454 g) pumpkin
3 spring onions
2 tomatoes
2 sprigs of thyme
ground black pepper

Method

Place the sweetcorn in a saucepan and cover with chicken stock.
Bring to the boil and allow to simmer gently.

Peel the pumpkin, remove the seeds, and dice it into 1 inch thick
cubes. Roughly chop the spring onions and tomatoes. Add these
vegetables to the saucepan along with the thyme and ground
black pepper (to taste).

Cook on a low heat for 30 minutes until the vegetables are soft.

Serving

Remove the tomato skin and thyme before serving.

Serves 6

Calories: 80 per portion

Breadfruit and Ackee Soup

Ingredients

1 lb breadfruit (454 g)
2 cloves garlic
a pinch of chilli powder
2 spring onions, 2 tomatoes
2 pints chicken stock
1 tin ackees (20 oz)

Method

Peel the garlic and chop finely. Peel the skin from the breadfruit, and cut into quarters. Remove the heart and cut the breadfruit wedges into small dice. Slice the tomatoes.

Pour the chicken stock and the chopped vegetables into a large saucepan. Bring to the boil and simmer on a low heat for 20 minutes — the breadfruit cubes should be tender at this point.

Pour away the brine and add the ackee segments to the saucepan. Bring back to boil, simmer for a further 5 minutes.

Liquidise the soup in a blender.

Serving

Serve with a pinch of chilli powder sprinkled on each portion.

Serves 4

Calories: 280 per portion

Caribbean Vegetable Soup

Ingredients

$\frac{1}{2}$ lb white yam
$\frac{1}{2}$ lb pumpkin
$\frac{1}{2}$ lb carrots, 4 tomatoes
$\frac{1}{2}$ lb sweetcorn (kernels)
$\frac{1}{2}$ lb sweet potato, 1 large cho cho
$\frac{1}{2}$ lb callaloo, 4 spring onions
2 cloves garlic, 2 pints chicken stock

Method

Peel the yam, sweet potato, and pumpkin. Remove the seeds and cut these vegetables into 2 inch thick cubes. Wash the callaloo, and chop roughly. Peel the carrots and cho cho and chop into wedges lengthways and then into 1 inch thick dice. Peel and chop the garlic, spring onions, and tomatoes.

Place the vegetables in a pot, pour in the chicken stock. Bring to the boil and simmer on a low heat for 20 minutes, then add the sweetcorn and cook for another 10 minutes.

Serving

Add a little ground black pepper or a pinch of chilli powder and stir well just before serving.

Serves 6

Calories: 200 per portion

MAIN COURSE DISHES

Main Course Fish

Notes on the Preparation of Fish

Grilled Mackerel

Poached Mullet

Fried Snapper

Grilled Snapper

Fried Mullet in Breadcrumbs

Grilled Mullet

Salted Fish Piquette

Poached Lobster

Main Course Meat

Notes on the Preparation of Meat

MAIN COURSE PORK

Caribbean Roast Pork

Jamaican Pork Stew

Spicy Grilled Pork Chops

Caribbean Baked Ham

MAIN COURSE CHICKEN

Chicken Caribbean

Chicken with Lime Sauce and Mango

MAIN COURSE BEEF

Grilled Steak with Spicy Butter Sauce

Grilled Steak with Caribbean Devilled Sauce

Grilled Rump Steak

Main Course Vegetables

Vegetarian Cakes

Crunchy Salad

Rice Salad

Vegetable Stew

Main Course Fish

Notes on the Preparation of Fish

Grilled Mackerel

Poached Mullet

Fried Snapper

Grilled Snapper

Fried Mullet

Grilled Mullet

Salted Fish Piquette

Poached Lobster

Notes on the Preparation of Fish

1. Scrape the scales from the fish with the back of a knife, scraping downwards from the tail fin to the head.

2. Cut away the head of the fish with a sharp knife.

3. Remove the intestines and trim away the fins.

4. Wash in cold water.

5. Pour a little vinegar and lime juice over the fish and leave to stand for a few minutes.

6. Drain then dry with a clean cloth.

7. Marinate in a mix of the following ingredients:

   2 cloves garlic finely chopped
   2 spring onions finely chopped
   6 pimento (berries) crushed
   salt and freshly ground black pepper
   1 sprig thyme
   1 teaspoon paprika
   juice of 1 lime

8. Spread the marinade mix over and inside the prepared, dried fish, using both hands. Cover with a lid or clean cloth and leave to stand for an hour before cooking.

Note: Wash hands thoroughly after using or preparing the marinade to remove all traces of pepper.

Grilled Mackerel

Ingredients

2 lb fresh mackerels, 1 lime (sliced)
4 oz vegetable margarine, 4 oz seasoned flour
4 tablespoons Caribbean Devilled Sauce

Method

Prepare the mackerels (see preparation of fish).

Coat the mackerels with the seasoned flour. Shake off the excess flour. Place on a greased baking tray and brush with the melted vegetable margarine. Spread the filleted mackerels on a grilling tray and grill under a hot grill for 5 minutes each side.

Serving

Serve on a dish with slices of lime and Caribbean Devilled Sauce.

Serves 4

Calories: 780 per portion

Suggested Accompaniments

Boiled Bananas and Butter Ackees

Note: Wash hands thoroughly after using marinade.

Poached Mullet

Ingredients

2 lb fresh mullet
4 tablespoons spicy butter sauce
1 lime (sliced)

Method

Prepare the mullets (see preparation of fish). Place the prepared mullets in a saucepan and add just enough water to cover. Bring to the boil and simmer on low heat for about 10 minutes. Turn each fish with a pallet knife, taking care to prevent them breaking, and simmer for a further 10 minutes.

Serving

Serve in the juices from the saucepan, a slice of lime and spicy butter sauce.

Serves 4

Calories: 525 per portion

Suggested Accompaniments

Boiled Cho Cho and Baby Sweetcorn

Fried Snapper

Ingredients

2 lb snapper fish (fresh), 4 oz seasoned flour
4 oz fresh breadcrumbs, 4 tablespoons Caribbean Devilled Sauce
1 lime (sliced), 1 egg, ¼ pint milk
vegetable oil for frying

Method

Break the egg into a bowl, add the milk and use a fork to whisk for 2-3 minutes. Coat the fishes with the seasoned flour — both sides — shaking away any excess flour.

Dip the fish into the egg and milk mixture then into the fresh breadcrumbs. Shake off the surplus breadcrumbs and deep fry to a golden brown, in a moderately hot oil (165°C) for approximately 5-6 minutes.

Serving

Serve with slices of lime and Caribbean Devilled Sauce.

Serves 4

Calories: 750 per portion

Suggested Accompaniments

Breadfruit Chips and Boiled Paw Paw

Grilled Snapper

Ingredients

2 lb snapper fish
4 oz vegetable margarine
4 oz seasoned flour, 1 lime (sliced)
4 tablespoons Spicy Butter Sauce
salt and pepper

Method

Prepare snapper (see preparation of fish) and sprinkle with salt and pepper to taste. Dust each fish with the seasoned flour, shaking away all surplus flour. Place the fishes on a greased baking tray, brush lightly with melted vegetable margarine and grill under a hot grill for 5 minutes each side.

Serving

Serve on a dish with slices of lime and Spicy Butter Sauce.

Serves 4

Calories: 730 per portion

Suggested Accompaniments

Green Salad

Fried Mullet

Ingredients

2 lb mullet fish
4 oz seasoned flour, 4 oz fresh breadcrumbs
4 tablespoons Caribbean Devilled Sauce
1 lime (sliced), 1 egg, $\frac{1}{4}$ pint milk
vegetable oil for frying

Method

Prepare the fish. Break the egg into a bowl, add the milk and
whisk vigorously with a fork for 2-3 minutes.

Coat the fishes in the seasoned flour and shake away any excess
to leave a thin coat. Dip each fish in the egg and milk mix, then
into the fresh breadcrumbs.

Deep fry to a golden brown, in a moderately hot oil
(165°C) for about 5-6 minutes.

Serving

Serve with slices of lime and Caribbean Devilled Sauce.

Serves 4

Calories: 720 per serving

Grilled Mullet

Ingredients

2 lb mullet fish, 1 sliced lime
2 oz vegetable margarine, 3 oz seasoned flour
4 tablespoons Spicy Butter Sauce

Method

Prepare the mullets by removing the head and intestines. Fillet each fish in the following manner: cut down along both sides of the backbone, remove the bone carefully, trim away the fins and excess rib bones.

Cover the mullet fillets with the seasoned flour. Shake off all the surplus flour to leave a thin coat on each fillet then place them side by side on a greased baking tray. Brush with melted vegetable margarine and grill on both sides under a hot grill for 5 minutes each side.

Serving

Serve with slices of lime and Spicy Butter Sauce.

Serves 4

Calories: 730 per portion

Suggested Accompaniments

Sweetcorn and Calalloo Salad

Salted Fish Piquette

Ingredients

1 lb salted fish
1 onion finely chopped, 1 egg yolk
a pinch of ground black pepper
juice of 1 lime, 4 oz melted butter
2 spring onions finely chopped

Method

Soak the saltfish for 5-6 hours in cold water. Flake then place in a greased ovenproof dish. Sprinkle with the chopped onions.

Beat the egg yolk and add the lime juice and black pepper; pour this mixture over the fish. Add the melted butter, cover dish and bake in a pre-heated, moderately hot oven (180°C or Gas Mark 4) for 20 minutes.

Serving

Serve with the juices from the bake with a sprinkling of chopped onions on each portion.

Serves 4

Calories: 470 per portion

Suggested Accompaniments

Boiled Bananas and Calalloo

Poached Lobster

Ingredients

2 lb fresh boiled lobster
1 pint wine vinegar, ¼ pint water
8 pimento berries, 1 onion
salt and pepper to taste

Method

Place the vinegar, water, pimento berries, and peeled, sliced onion in a large saucepan with the boiled lobster, cover, bring to the boil then allow to simmer on a low heat for 15-25 minutes, allow to cool in the cooking liquor.

Detach the claws and joints, crack and remove the meat in whole pieces, if possible. Cut the lobster in half with a large knife, to separate head. Cut through the centre of the tail and remove the meat. Cut through the head portion and remove the meat with a small knife.

Serving

Add salt and pepper to taste.

Serves 4

Calories: 285 per portion

Suggested Accompaniments

Green Salad

Main Course Meat

Notes on the Preparation of Meat

MAIN COURSE PORK

Caribbean Roast Pork

Jamaican Pork Stew

Spicy Grilled Pork Chops

Caribbean Baked Ham

MAIN COURSE CHICKEN

Chicken Caribbean

Chicken with Lime Sauce and Mango

MAIN COURSE BEEF

Grilled Steak with Spicy Butter Sauce

Grilled Steak with Caribbean Devilled Sauce

Grilled Rump Steak

Notes on the Preparation of Meat

1. Trim away excess fat.

2. Wash well in cold water.

3. Drain and dry with a clean cloth.

4. Make 3 or 4 light incisions into the meat with a sharp knife.

5. Prepare marinade of the following ingredients:

   2 cloves garlic, finely chopped
   6 pimento (allspice) berries crushed finely
   4 tablespoons soya sauce, 4 spring onions chopped
   freshly ground black pepper, salt, $\frac{1}{2}$ teaspoon ground clove
   1 teaspoon paprika, 1 teaspoon soft brown sugar
   $\frac{1}{2}$ teaspoon of thinly sliced root ginger.

   Put all the ingredients in a bowl and mix.

6. Place the meat in the bowl with the marinade mix and rub in with the fingers, using both hands. Cover and leave to stand in a cool place for 2 to 3 hours before cooking.

   Meat can be left to stand in this marinade for up to 12 hours before cooking.

Main Course Pork

Caribbean Roast Pork

Ingredients

2 lb loin of pork, 2 tablespoons soft brown sugar
2 oz butter, $\frac{1}{4}$ teaspoon powdered cloves
2 cloves garlic (chopped finely), 2 tablespoons salt
$\frac{1}{2}$ red sweet pepper (chopped), 1 tablespoon lime juice
6 pimento berries (crushed), 1 sprig thyme

Method

Wash and dry the pork and rub the salt thoroughly over it with the fingers. Cover with a clean cloth then leave to stand in a cool place for 20 minutes. Rub the garlic, cloves, pimento and thyme into the incisions. Baste with the butter and put onto a roasting tray, uncovered, in a moderately hot oven (180°C, Gas Mark 4). Bake for 25 minutes turning and basting with the juices.

Pull roasting tray from the oven and sprinkle the sugar over the roast, then raise the oven temperature to Gas Mark 6 (200°C) and bake for another 30 minutes.

Serving

Cut into slices and serve with Paw Paw Sauce.

Serves 4

Calories: 820 per portion

Jamaican Pork Stew

Ingredients

4 pork chops (2 lb), 1 tablespoon vinegar, 1 green mango
1 tablespoon lime juice, 4 tablespoons soya sauce, 1 cho cho
$\frac{1}{2}$ teaspoon root ginger, 1 lb pumpkin (sliced)
1 lb green bananas, 1 pint vegetable stock
1 lb yam, 2 tablespoons corn flour, 6 pimento berries (crushed)
2 cloves garlic (chopped), 4 spring onions (chopped)
2 tablespoons vegetable oil, 1 teaspoon brown sugar

Method

Peel the bananas, cut each into four slices lengthways then across
the length of each slice. Peel the cho cho, cut it into wedges and
remove the heart. Remove the seeds from the pumpkin, then peel
and chop coarsely. Peel the yam and cut it into thick slices. Peel
the mango and cut the flesh into slices. Place these vegetables in a
large roasting pan, add vegetable oil and place pan on a low heat.
Add the garlic, pimento, spring onions, root ginger, and stir well.
Cook without colour for five minutes, add the vegetable stock and
bring back to the boil. Add the sugar, thyme, vinegar, soya sauce
and the prepared pork chops to the pan. Cover and place it in the
oven at Gas Mark 4 (180°C) for 1 hour.

Serving

Serve hot with a slice of wholemeal bread.

Serves 4

Calories: 780 per serving

Spicy Grilled Pork Chops

Ingredients

4 pork chops (2 lb), 4 tablespoons soya sauce
6 pimento berries crushed finely, salt and pepper
4 tablespoons paw paw sauce, 1 clove garlic chopped finely
2 oz seasoned flour, 2 oz melted margarine

Method

Trim the excess fat from the chops. Wash well and dry with a clean cloth. Place the pork chops in a bowl. Add salt and pepper to taste, pimento, soya sauce, the chopped garlic and rub these into the meat with the fingers.

Cover, stand in a cool place for 1 hour, then remove the chops and shake to remove excess liquid. Coat the chops with the seasoned flour, shaking away any excess, and place them on a greased baking tray. Brush with the margarine and grill on both sides under a hot grill for 5 minutes each side.

Serving

Serve with paw paw sauce.

Serves 4

Calories: 590 per portion

Suggested Accompaniments

Yam Chips and Boiled Paw Paw.

Caribbean Baked Ham

Ingredients

2 lb ham, 2 tablespoons honey
8 whole cloves, 3 tablespoons soft brown sugar
4 pimento berries crushed

Method

Place the ham in a saucepan with just enough water to cover and bring to the boil. Simmer on a gentle heat for 50 minutes. Allow to cool in the liquid. Rub the pimento in and around the ham.

Place in a roasting tray and bake in a slow oven for 20 minutes. Remove from the oven and score across the rind in the shape of diamonds. Insert the whole cloves into scores made in the rind then pour over the honey to cover. Sprinkle with the brown sugar then return to the oven at Gas Mark 3 (160°C) and bake for 30 minutes until golden.

Serving

Cut into slices and serve hot or cold.

Serves 4

Calories: 720 per portion

Suggested Accompaniments

Boiled Baby Sweetcorn and Boiled Yam

Main Course Chicken

Chicken Caribbean

Ingredients

3 lb fresh whole chicken
2 oz vegetable margarine, juice of one lime
4 tablespoons Caribbean Devilled Sauce

Method

Remove the wishbone then place the bird on its back. Insert a large knife through the neck and out of the rear vent. Cut through the backbone and open flat. Wash well with the lime juice and dry with a clean cloth. Brush with the margarine then place on a flat baking tray under the grill.

Cook under the grill for 20 minutes each side, brushing every five minutes with margarine. Pierce the drumstick with a fork, there should be no sign of blood when cooked.

Serving

Serve with Caribbean Devilled Sauce.

Serves 4

Calories: 670 per serving

Suggested Accompaniments

Baby Sweetcorn, Boiled Cho Cho and Boiled Yam

Chicken with Lime Sauce and Mango

Ingredients

3 lb fresh chicken
2 oz vegetable margarine
4 tablespoons lime sauce
juice of one lime

Method

Remove the wishbone. Place the chicken on its back, insert a large knife through the neck end and out of the vent. Cut through the backbone and open flat. Wash well with the lime juice and dry with a clean cloth. Brush the chicken with a little melted vegetable margarine. Place the well seasoned chicken on a pre-heated greased grill (low heat) or on a flat baking tray under the grill. Brush with the margarine frequently during cooking. Allow approximately 15-20 minutes each side. Pierce the drumstick with a fork or pointed knife — there should be no sign of blood issuing from the leg when cooked.

Serving

Serve with boiled green mango and lime sauce and salad.

Calories: 710 per serving

Main Course Beef

Grilled Steak with Spicy Butter Sauce

Ingredients

2 lb fillet steak (cut into 4 slices, round)
2 oz vegetable margarine
4 tablespoons Spicy Butter Sauce

Method

Trim off all fat from the steaks then flatten with a mallet. Place steaks on a flat baking tray under the grill, and grill for approximately 5-10 minutes on each side. Brush on both sides with melted margarine and continue cooking to taste.

Serving

Serve with Spicy Butter Sauce.

Serves 4

Calories: 580 per serving

Suggested Accompaniments

Coco Chips and choice of salad

Grilled Steak with Caribbean Devilled Sauce

Ingredients

2 lb sirloin steak (4 half-pound steaks)
2 oz vegetable margarine
4 tablespoons Caribbean Devilled Sauce

Method

Trim off all excess fat from the steaks then flatten with a mallet. Place the steaks on a flat baking tray under the grill. Brush on both sides with melted margarine and cook, to the degree of your choice.

Serving

Serve with Caribbean Devilled Sauce.

Serves 4

Calories: 580 per portion

Suggested Accompaniments

Banana Chips, Butter Ackees and choice of salad

Grilled Rump Steak

Ingredients

2 lb rump steaks
2 oz vegetable margarine

Method

Trim off all excess fat from the steaks then flatten with a mallet or cutlet bat. Place the steaks on greased grill bars, preheated on low heat. Brush on both sides with melted margarine and cook both sides, to the degree of your choice.

Serving

Serve directly from the grill.

Serves 4

Calories: 560 per portion

Suggested Accompaniments

Yam Chips and Boiled Cho Cho

Main Course Vegetables

Vegetarian Cakes

Crunchy Salad

Rice Salad

Vegetable Stew

Vegetarian Cakes

Ingredients

2 green bananas, 1 cho cho
3 oz sweetcorn (kernels), 2 lb white yam
2 spring onions, 4 tablespoons milk (soya)
2 eggs, 4 oz wholemeal flour, 8 oz breadcrumbs
vegetable oil for frying, salt and pepper to taste

Method

Peel and wash the yam and bananas then cut into thin slices.
Peel the cho cho, cut it into wedges and remove the heart.
Bring a large saucepan of water to the boil, add the sliced yam,
cho cho, sweetcorn and bananas, cover and simmer on a low heat
for about 20-30 minutes, then pour away the water. Puree the
yam but leave the bananas, sweetcorn and cho cho aside to cool.
Chop the spring onions very finely. Place the yam and spring
onions in a mixing bowl, add one egg yolk, salt and freshly
ground black pepper. Mix well with a wooden spoon then
gradually add the cold cooked banana, sweetcorn and cho cho to
the yam mixture while stirring. Remove the resultant dough in
small portions and form into small balls. Break the remaining egg
in a mixing bowl, add the milk and stir well. Roll the vegetable
balls through the flour to coat, dip each into the beaten egg then
roll in the breadcrumbs to cover. Flatten the balls slightly then
deep fry in hot vegetable oil at 185°C until golden brown. Drain
to remove any excess oil.

Serves 4

Calories: 480 per portion

Crunchy Salad

Ingredients

2 tablespoons wine vinegar
2 tablespoons clear honey
2 tablespoons soya sauce
2 tablespoons vegetable oil
2 cloves garlic crushed, 1 onion finely chopped
2 green and red peppers, 12 oz white cabbage
$1/2$ bunch fresh radish

Method

De-seed and cut the peppers into strips, shred the cabbage and cut the radish into thin slices. Mix the vinegar, honey and soya sauce.

Heat the oil in a frying pan and stir fry the garlic and onion for 1 minute. Add the pepper and cabbage and stir fry for a further 5 minutes. Add the radishes and cook for 1 minute then stir the vinegar mixture into the vegetables.

Serving

Pour directly onto serving dishes, allow to cool before serving.

Serves 6

Calories: 135 per portion

Note: Avoid overcooking the vegetables.

Rice Salad

Ingredients

2 fl oz freshly squeezed orange juice
2 tablespoons vegetable oil, 2 tablespoons soya sauce
2 oz sultanas, 8 oz brown rice cooked and cooled
2 oz beansprouts, 1 green pepper de-seeded and chopped
2 spring onions (chopped), 2 oz roasted cashew nuts
1 stick celery (chopped), salt and pepper to taste

Method

To make the dressing, combine the freshly squeezed orange juice,
vegetable oil and soya sauce and add salt and pepper to taste.

Bring a small pan of water to the boil, add the sultanas, simmer
for about 2 minutes then drain. Allow to cool, mix in the
remaining ingredients then pour the dressing over the salad and
mix well with a wooden spoon.

Serving

Chill slightly before serving. Garnish with a little chilli powder or
paprika.

Serves 6

Calories: 275 per portion

Vegetable Stew

Ingredients

1 lb carrots, 1 lb callaloo, 2 lb white yam
2 spring onions, 2 peppers (1 red and 1 green)
6 pimento berries, $\frac{1}{2}$ lb grated red Leicester cheese
salt and pepper, 2 vegetable stock cubes
2 pints water, 1 clove garlic, 1 lb cho cho

Method

Chop the callaloo and remove any yellow bits. Quarter the peppers, remove the seeds then dice. Peel the cho cho, cut it into wedges and remove the heart. Crush the pimento berries and garlic. Peel the yam and carrots, cut it into thin slices.

Add the vegetable stock to two pints of hot water in a large oven-proof dish; add the carrots, callaloo, peppers, spring onions, pimento berries, cho cho, garlic, salt and pepper then arrange the slices of yam on top. The stock should just cover the vegetables. Sprinkle with the grated cheese, cover and place in a hot oven Gas Mark 6 (200°C) for 30 minutes. Remove the lid then leave in the oven for a further 10 minutes.

Serving

Garnish with chopped parsley.

Serves 4

Calories: 630 per portion

ACCOMPANIMENTS

White Yam Frittes

Breadfruit Chips

Green Banana Chips

Coco Chips

Cream Yam

Boiled Green Bananas

Boiled Baby Sweetcorn

Boiled Cho Cho

Butter Ackees

Boiled Sweet Potatoes

Boiled Green Paw Paw

White Yam Frittes

Ingredients

2 lb white yams
vegetable oil for frying
salt and pepper

Method

Peel the yams, wash then cut into approximately $\frac{1}{2}$ inch thick slices. Cut each slice across to make sticks approximately 2 inches long. Dry these yam sticks with a drying cloth then cook in a frying basket in moderately hot oil (165°C).

Remove from fryer before the yam sticks start to colour and drain to remove any excess frying oil. Leave standing on a paper towel, which should absorb excess oil, until required.

When required place in a frying basket at 185°C and cook until crisp and golden.

Drain well then season with salt and pepper.

Serving

Serve on a dish lined with paper.

Serves 4

Calories: 360 per serving

Breadfruit Chips

Ingredients

$^1/_2$ breadfruit (1 lb)
vegetable oil for frying
salt and pepper

Method

Peel the breadfruit, cut into quarters and remove the heart.
Wash well, then cut into slices $^1/_2$ inch thick and 2 inches long.
Cut the slices into long strips roughly $^1/_2$ inch in width. Wash the
strips and then dry with a cloth.

Cook in a frying basket in moderately hot oil (165°C). Remove
before chips start to colour and drain, then place on a paper
kitchen towel until required.

When needed return these to the frying basket and cook in hot oil
(185°C) until crisp and golden.

Serving

Add salt and pepper to taste.

Serves 4

Calories: 190 per serving

Green Banana Chips

Ingredients

4 green bananas (1 lb)
vegetable oil

Method

Slice the ends of each banana, cut them into two halves across then peel and discard skins. Cut the banana into thin slices, wash well and dry.

Heat the oil in a frying pan and when hot add the banana slices and fry until they are a golden brown.

Serving

Spread chips on a paper towel to remove oil then add salt and pepper to taste.

Serves 4

Calories: 160 per serving

Hint: Banana chips can be served alone as an appetiser or as accompaniment to meat or fish dishes.

Coco Chips

Ingredients

4 medium sized cocos (1 lb)
vegetable oil
salt and pepper

Method

Peel the cocos, wash then cut into ½ inch thick slices.

Cut each slice across to make sticks approximately 2 inches long.

Dry these sticks with a drying cloth then cook in a frying basket in moderately hot oil (165°C).

Remove from fryer before the chips start to colour and drain to remove any excess frying oil and leave standing on a paper towel to absorb excess oil until required.

When required place in a frying basket at 185°C and cook until crisp and golden. Drain well then season with salt and pepper.

Serving

Serve on a dish lined with paper.

Serves 4

Calories: 340 per portion

Cream Yam

Ingredients

2 lb white yams
3 oz butter, 6 tablespoons milk
a pinch of freshly ground nutmeg
salt and pepper, juice of one lime
chopped parsley

Method

Peel and wash the yam. Cut into $\frac{1}{2}$ inch thick slices. Place the yam slices in a pot, add water to cover. Bring to boil and cook until the slices are soft (15 minutes). Add salt to taste then allow to simmer on a low heat until the yam is very soft (5-10 minutes). Drain away the water. Replace the lid on the saucepan and return to a low heat to remove excess water but do not allow to dry completely. Add the other ingredients and stir with a wooden spoon, stirring continuously until the mixture has a smooth creamy consistency.

Serving

Add a sprinkle of chopped parsley.

Serves 4

Calories: 400 per serving

Hint: An excellent substitute for mashed potatoes.

Boiled Green Bananas

Ingredients

4 green bananas

Method

Bring a large saucepan of water to the boil. Cut the ends off the bananas and score them along the length, cutting to the flesh. Add them to the pan of boiling water and boil for 25 minutes.

Allow time to cool then remove the bananas from the water (do not allow the water to get cold) and peel away the skins.

Serving

Serve with a little melted butter.

Serves 4

Calories: 110 per serving

Note: The skins can be removed from the bananas before cooking but this is considerably more difficult — cooking in the skin also preserves the flavour and prevents leaching of iron from the banana. Green bananas have a high iron content.

Boiled Baby Sweetcorn

Ingredients

1 lb baby sweetcorn
4 oz butter
salt and pepper

Method

Wash the sweetcorn, cut each cob into two, lengthways, and place the halves in a saucepan of boiling water. Use enough water to just cover the sweetcorn, simmer on a low heat for 20 minutes, until the sweetcorn is tender.

Pour away the water and add butter, a sprinkling of salt and pepper to taste and stir.

Serving

Serve hot, or cold with a spicy dressing.

Serves 4

Calories: 60 per serving

Hint: Served cold, it makes a delicious addition to salads.

Boiled Cho Cho

Ingredients

4 medium-sized cho cho (1 lb)
2 oz melted butter
salt and pepper

Method

Peel the cho cho and cut into wedges, lengthways. Cut away and discard the fibrous heart tissue then place the wedges into a saucepan with just enough water to cover.

Bring the water to the boil, add the butter, salt and pepper to taste. Simmer on a low heat for 15-20 minutes until the cho cho is soft.

Serving

Serve with juices (hot).

Serves 4

Calories: 50 per serving

Hint: Cho cho makes an ideal substitute for courgettes but has a more delicate flavour.

Butter Ackees

Ingredients

1 clove garlic
1 large tin ackees (20 oz) in brine
4 oz butter
salt and pepper
2 spring onions

Method

Heat the butter in a saucepan on gentle heat. Chop the garlic and spring onions finely. Add these to the oil in the saucepan and cook on a gentle heat without colour.

Drain the ackees and add them to the contents of the saucepan, stirring with a wooden spoon to avoid colouring, while taking care not to break the ackee segments.

Serving

Serve when hot.

Serves 4

Calories: 210 per portion

Hints: Ackees have a consistency similar to scrambled eggs and a very delicate flavour and can be served with either fish or meat.

Boiled Sweet Potatoes

Ingredients

2 lb sweet potatoes

Method

Peel and wash the potatoes then cut into wedges and place into a large saucepan with just enough water to cover. Bring to boil and allow to simmer on gentle heat for 20-30 minutes until soft.

Serving

Serve hot.

Serves 4

Calories: 220 per serving

Note: Sweet potatoes have a consistency similar to the potato. There are however several varieties which differ slightly in flavour, colour and texture when cooked.

Boiled Green Paw Paw

Ingredients

4 medium-sized green paw paw (2 lb)
salt and pepper

Method

Peel the paw paw and cut into wedges. Remove the seeds and place the segments in a large saucepan with just enough water to cover. Bring to boil and simmer on low heat for 10-15 minutes until the paw paw segments are soft. Drain away the liquid and add salt and pepper to taste.

Serving

Serve hot.

Serves 4

Calories: 110 per serving

SALADS

Banana and Orange Salad

Paw Paw and Sweetcorn Salad

Yam and Cucumber Salad

Breadfruit and Ackee Salad

Cho Cho and Cashew Nut Salad

Sweetcorn and Callaloo Salad

Green Salad

Cashew Nut and Mango Salad

Sweetcorn and Apple Salad

Mango and Tomato Salad

Sweet Potato Salad

Green Banana and Cho Cho Salad

Banana and Orange Salad

Ingredients

2 large oranges
2 lb firm ripe bananas
a bunch of watercress
juice of 1 lime

Method

Peel all the leaves off the watercress, wash well and drain.
Peel and discard the skin and pith of the oranges then cut them
into thin slices (round). Peel the bananas and cut into slices about
1 inch thick.

Serving

Place the orange, banana, watercress, and lime juice into a salad
bowl and stir well.

Serves 4

Calories: 260 per portion

Paw Paw and Sweetcorn Salad

Ingredients

2 medium-sized ripe paw paw
1 lb baby sweetcorn
2 tablespoons low calorie dressing

Method

Wash the sweetcorn and drain then cut each cob into halves lengthways and place them in a saucepan with just enough water to cover.

Bring to the boil and simmer on a low heat for 15 minutes until the sweetcorn is tender. Allow to cool (cold water can be added to pan to speed cooling). Pour away the water and transfer corn to a salad bowl.

Peel and cut the paw paw into wedges, remove the seeds, dice and add to the sweetcorn. Mix well by stirring with a wooden spoon. Add the dressing and stir well.

Serves 4

Calories: 110 per portion

Yam and Cucumber Salad

Ingredients

1 lb yam
1 cucumber
2 tablespoons spicy dressing
1 large beef tomato

Method

Peel the yam, wash in cold water then cut into 1 inch thick cubes.
Place the yam in a saucepan with just enough water to cover and
bring to boil. Cover and simmer on low heat for 20 minutes or
until the yam is soft.

Allow to cool (cold water can be added to speed cooling).
When cool, drain well.

Peel and dice the cucumber then put it into a salad bowl, add the
yam and salad dressing and stir well with a wooden spoon.

Serving

Cut the tomato into round thin slices and place decoratively on
top of the salad.

Serves 4

Calories: 195 per portion

Breadfruit and Ackee Salad

Ingredients

2 lb breadfruit
4 tablespoons spicy salad dressing
1 large tin of ackees in brine (20 oz)
$\frac{1}{2}$ teaspoon paprika

Method

Peel and quarter the breadfruit, cutting from stem to base, then remove the heart (fibrous central portion) from the quarters. Cut each segment into 3 pieces.

Bring 1 pint of water to the boil in a pot, add the breadfruit pieces and bring back to boil. Cover and allow to simmer for 20 minutes until the breadfruit is tender.

Remove pan from the heat, allow to cool then place the breadfruit pieces in a salad bowl.

Add the ackees (the brine should be poured away) to the breadfruit. Add the dressing and stir well with a wooden spoon.

Serving

Add a sprinkle of paprika on top of each portion.

Serves 4

Calories: 245 per portion

Cho Cho and Cashew Nut Salad

Ingredients

4 medium sized cho cho (2 lb)
4 oz unsalted cashew nuts
4 tablespoons low calorie dressing
a pinch of salt and pepper
chopped parsley to decorate

Method

Peel the cho cho, cut into wedges lengthways and remove the heart. Dice and place in a saucepan with just enough water to cover.

Bring to the boil, cover and simmer on a gentle heat for 15-20 minutes until the cho cho is soft.

Allow to cool, then drain and place the cho cho in a salad bowl. Add the cashew nuts, low calorie dressing, salt and pepper to taste and stir well with a wooden spoon.

Serving

Decorate with a sprinkle of chopped parsley.

Serves 4

Calories: 170 per portion

Sweetcorn and Callaloo Salad

Ingredients

1 lb baby sweetcorn
1 lb callaloo, salt and pepper
4 tablespoons spicy dressing
a pinch of paprika

Method

Wash the sweet corn then cut each ear into halves, lengthways and place them in a saucepan, with just enough water to cover.

Bring to the boil and simmer on a low heat for 15 minutes until the sweetcorn is tender. Allow to cool and drain.

Wash and drain the callaloo then remove the larger and older stems. Chop coarsely and place in a saucepan with just enough water to cover. Bring to boil and simmer for 15 minutes. Allow to cool and drain well.

Place the callaloo and sweetcorn in a salad bowl. Add salt and pepper, spicy dressing and stir with a wooden spoon to mix.

Serving

Decorate with a spinkling of paprika.

Serves 4

Calories: 78 per portion

Green Salad

Ingredients

2 large cucumbers
2 medium-sized green peppers (sweet)
6 tablespoons spicy dressing
2 spring onions finely chopped
a pinch of salt and pepper

Method

Cut the peppers into quarters, remove and discard the seeds then cut each quarter into thin slices. Peel and dice the cucumbers.

Place the peppers and cucumbers into a salad bowl, add the spicy salad dressing, the finely chopped spring onions, a pinch of salt and pepper and mix well with a wooden spoon.

Serving

Serve chilled.

Serves 4

Calories: 56 per portion

Cashew Nut and Mango Salad

Ingredients

4 medium-sized green mangoes
4 oz unsalted cashew nuts
4 tablespoons spicy dressing
a pinch of chilli powder

Method

Peel the mangoes and cut away the flesh from the central stone in slices.

Place the mango slices into a salad bowl. Add the cashew nuts and spicy dressing. Stir well with a wooden spoon, adding just a pinch of chilli powder.

Serving

Serve chilled.

Serves 4

Calories: 245 per portion

Hint: Excellent accompaniment to meat dishes.

Sweetcorn and Apple Salad

Ingredients

4 eating apples, 1 lb baby sweetcorn
4 tablespoons low calorie dressing, 1 tablespoon honey
1 tablespoon lime juice

Method

Wash the sweetcorn then cut each ear into halves lengthways and place them in a saucepan with just enough water to cover.

Bring to the boil and simmer on a low heat for 15 minutes until the sweetcorn is tender. Allow to cool and drain.

Peel the apples and cut into wedges. Remove the heart and seeds.

Place the apple wedges into a bowl, pour in the lime juice and stir well for about 1 minute. Drain well. Add the sweetcorn, low calorie dressing and 1 tablespoon honey, and mix well with a wooden spoon until the dressing coats the apple pieces.

Serving

Serve with fish or meat or on its own.

Serves 4

Calories: 87 per portion

Mango and Tomato Salad

Ingredients

4 medium-sized green mangoes
1 lb salad tomatoes, 6 tablespoons spicy dressing
1 teaspoon soft brown sugar

Method

Peel the mangoes and cut away the flesh from the central stone in slices. Place the mango slices into a salad bowl.

Wash and cut the tomatoes in slices (round). Add these to the mango slices along with the spicy dressing and soft brown sugar. Mix well with a wooden spoon.

Serving

Allow the salad to stand for at least 1 hour before serving.

Serves 4

Calories: 155 per portion

Sweet Potato Salad

Ingredients

2 lb sweet potatoes
4 tablespoons spicy dressing
1 lb salad tomatoes
1 spring onion finely chopped

Method

Peel the potatoes, wash and cut into 1 inch dice and place in a saucepan with just enough water to cover. Bring to the boil and simmer on a low heat for 15-20 minutes. Drain away the water and leave to cool.

When cold, place the diced potatoes into a salad bowl and add the spicy dressing and finely chopped spring onion. Stir well with a wooden spoon.

Wash and cut the tomatoes and slice thinly (round) and place slices decoratively on the salad.

Serving

Chill well before serving.

Serves 4

Calories: 225 per portion

Green Banana and Cho Cho Salad

Ingredients

4 green bananas
4 medium-sized cho cho
4 tablespoons spicy dressing

Method

Peel the cho cho, cut into wedges lengthways and remove the heart. Dice into 1 inch thick cubes. Place the cho cho cubes in a saucepan with just enough water to cover. Bring to the boil and simmer on a low heat for 15-20 minutes until soft. Allow to cool and drain well.

Bring a large pot of water to the boil. Cut and discard the ends of the bananas then score each through the skin deeply along their length. Add the bananas to the pot of boiling water, bring back to boil and cook for 25 minutes. Drain well and leave to cool. When cold cut the bananas into 3 slices lengthways, then across the length twice.

Mix the cho cho and banana slices in a salad bowl with the spicy dressing.

Serves 6

Calories: 180 per portion

SALAD
DRESSINGS

Spicy Salad Dressing

Low Calorie Salad Dressing

Spicy Salad Dressing

Ingredients

$^1/_4$ pint wine vinegar
$^1/_4$ pint olive oil, 1 clove garlic chopped finely
$^1/_2$ teaspoon dried mixed herbs, 1 tablespoon honey
6 pimento berries (allspice) crushed finely
a pinch of salt, a pinch of ground black pepper
1 teaspoon paprika, 1 teaspoon dried mustard
1 tablespoon lime juice

Method

Place the vinegar in a large saucepan and heat gently to boiling.
Remove from the heat and put aside to cool.

When cold add all the other ingredients to the vinegar. Mix well
with a wooden spoon.

Cover and keep into a cool place for at least one hour before
serving.

Serves 16

Calories: 90 per portion

Low Calorie Salad Dressing

Ingredients

$1/2$ teaspoon chopped parsley
$1/2$ pint natural yogurt
2 spring onions chopped finely
ground black pepper, a pinch of salt
$1/2$ teaspoon paprika

Method

Place the yogurt into a mixing bowl then add the finely chopped spring onions and stir well with a wooden spoon. Add the ground black pepper, salt, parsley – finely chopped – and the paprika, stirring well to blend the ingredients into the yogurt mix.

Serving

Serve when required. Keep in a cool place.

Serves 10

Calories: 25 per portion

Note: This salad dressing is a substitute for mayonnaise.

DESSERTS

Lime Francosse

Lemon and Coconut Candies

Apple Peekala

Paw Paw Pudding

Summer Candies Pudding

Bananas Sarah Bernard

Honeycomb Simba

Vanilla Bavrios

Brandy Delight

Cinnamon and Honey Fluff

Tropical Fruit Mousse

Honey Baked Stuffed Apples

Caribbean Currants Sorbet

Paw Paw Sundae

Orange and Coconut Fluff

Lime Francosse

Ingredients

1 egg
1 oz butter
6 oz brown sugar
3 tablespoons lime juice
grated rind from one lime
a pinch of ground nutmeg for decorating

Method

Place a bowl over a small pan of hot water. Break the egg into the
bowl and whisk. Add the lime rind, sugar, lime juice and butter.
Bring the water to boil and cook the mixture, while stirring,
for 3 minutes.

Serving

Allow to cool and decorate with a sprinkle of ground nutmeg
when serving.

Serves 2

Calories: 430 per portion

Lemon and Coconut Candies

Ingredients

4 oz wholemeal flour
$\frac{1}{2}$ teaspoon vanilla essence, 4 oz butter
desiccated coconut (for decorating)
a pinch of salt, 1 oz icing sugar, 4 tablespoons lemon curd

Method

Mix the flour and salt and shake through a fine sieve to remove
any large particles from the wholemeal. Place the butter, sugar
and essence of vanilla in a small bowl and cream. Add the flour to
the bowl gradually while stirring and mix well to make a
consistent dough. Take one tablespoon at a time of dough (one
for each candy), and roll this into a small ball in the palm of the
hand – the mixture should be sufficient for six. Flatten the ball of
dough slightly. Place the doughballs an inch apart on an
ungreased baking tray.

Bake in a moderately hot oven (200°C, Gas Mark 6) until lightly
browned. Allow to cool.

Serving

Cover each candy with lemon curd then add a sprinkling of
desiccated coconut before serving.

Serves 6

Calories: 205 per portion

Apple Peekala

Ingredients

1 lb cooking apples
$1/2$ pint cold water, 2 oz brown sugar
6 oz self raising flour, $1/4$ teaspoon mixed spices
3 oz shredded beef suet, juice of $1/2$ a lime

Method

Mix and sieve the flour and spices, add the suet and grated rind and mix to a stiff dough with water. Shape the dough into 15 balls.

Peel and slice the apples. Remove the core. Pour the water into a saucepan, add the apple slices, lime juice and sugar and bring to the boil.

When all traces of the sugar have dissolved, drop the balls into the saucepan. Cover and allow to cook gently for 15 minutes.

Serving

Drain and serve with natural yogurt or honey.

Serves 15

Calories: 96 per portion

Paw Paw Pudding

Ingredients

4 medium-sized ripe paw paw ($^1/_2$ lb)
$^1/_2$ pint water
8 oz brown sugar
$^1/_2$ pint natural yogurt
a pinch of freshly ground ginger

Method

Peel and cut the paw paw into wedges lengthways. Remove the seeds. Place the paw paw and water in a large saucepan, bring to the boil and simmer gently for 20 minutes, the paw paw slices should at this time be very soft.

Remove from heat, cool and then blend. Slowly add the sugar, mixing well with a wooden spoon then place the mixture in a refrigerator for a few minutes to chill.

Whip the yogurt and add this to the paw paw puree with a spoon, folding (not mixing) it into the puree.

Serving

Pour into individual glasses and serve cold. Decorate with a tablespoon of honey in each glass.

Serves 4

Calories: 630 per portion

Summer Candies Pudding

Ingredients

1 packet strawberry jelly
2 tablespoons brown sugar, 6 slices brown bread
1 lb mixed fruit – ripe banana and pineapple slices

Method

Dissolve jelly in a small amount ($\frac{1}{4}$ pint) of hot water. Add cold water to make $\frac{3}{4}$ pint.

Cut away the crust from the bread and arrange about four slices, breaking as necessary, to cover the bottom and sides of a $1\frac{1}{2}$ pint dessert bowl. Spoon enough of the dissolved jelly over the bread until it is soaked. Add the fruit mix and sugar to $\frac{1}{4}$ pint water in a saucepan, bring to the boil and cook until the fruit is very soft.

Stir the remaining jelly into the stewed fruit and leave to cool. Before the jelly sets pour it into the bread lined bowl. Use the remaining bread to cover, pressing the slices into the jelly mixture. Leave in a cool place until set.

Serving

Turn out and serve with honey or natural yogurt.

Serves 6

Calories: 105 per portion

Bananas Sarah Bernard

Ingredients

1 packet raspberry jelly
2 firm ripe bananas, $1/2$ pint natural yogurt
2 medium paw paw (ripe)

Method

Peel and cut the paw paw into slices. Remove the seeds and place the slices in a saucepan. Add enough cold water to cover and bring to the boil. Cover and simmer on gentle heat for 15 minutes.

Dissolve the jelly in a small amount of hot water then make up to $3/4$ pint with cold water. Leave until cool and almost to the point of setting. Whisk in the yogurt. Peel and cut the banana into slices and add these along with the boiled paw paw slices to the jelly, stirring slowly with a wooden spoon to distribute evenly. Pour into 4 individual dishes and leave to set.

Serving

Decorate each dish with the remaining banana slices and serve at once.

Serves 4

Calories: 120 per portion

Hint: To prevent the banana slices from going brown, sprinkle with lemon or orange juice.

Honeycomb Simba

Ingredients

1 packet strawberry jelly, 2 eggs
$1/2$ pint milk (soya), 6 wholemeal biscuits

Method

Dissolve the jelly in $1/4$ pint hot water.

Warm the milk.

Separate the yolks and whites of the eggs. Whisk the yolks to a creamy and thick consistency then gradually stir in the milk. Pour into a large saucepan and simmer over a gentle heat while stirring until the mixture thickens. Remove from the heat, pour into a large bowl and gradually stir in the jelly.

Whisk the egg whites until stiff, then fold (avoid mixing) into the jelly and pour into a $1^1/2$ pint mould and leave to set.

Serving

Turn out onto a plate and serve with wholemeal biscuits.

Serves 6

Calories: 110 per portion

Vanilla Bavrios

Ingredients

1 pint milk
2 tablespoons vanilla essence
2 tablespoons hot water, 2 eggs
1 oz brown sugar, 15g gelatine

Method

Separate the egg yolks, add the sugar and vanilla essence to the yolks and milk, whisk then cook on a low heat without boiling. When mixture starts to thicken, remove from the heat.

Dissolve the gelatine in the hot water and stir this into the egg yolk mixture. Allow to cool.

Whisk the egg whites until stiff and fold into mixture then pour into a serving dish or mould and allow to set.

Serving

Chill well before serving.

Serves 4

Calories: 180 per portion

Brandy Delight

Ingredients

5 fl oz ($^1/_4$ pint) strong coffee
3 tablespoons brown sugar or honey
8 oz natural yogurt
1 tablespoon brandy, 8g gelatine
6 tablespoons water

Method

Bring the coffee to the boil, add the water then sprinkle in the gelatine, stirring until it dissolves.

Pour into a bowl and leave to cool but not set.

Stir in the yogurt, the sugar (or honey) and the brandy then whisk to a fluffy consistency.

Serving

Pour into individual glasses and refrigerate until set.

Serves 4

Calories: 75 per portion

Cinnamon and Honey Fluff

Ingredients

4 dessert apples (1$\frac{1}{2}$ lb)
2 tablespoons redcurrant jelly
a pinch of ground cinnamon
juice of one lime, 2 egg whites
2 tablespoons honey

Method

Peel and core the apples then dice. Place in a saucepan and cook
in a small amount of water until very soft. Liquidise then add the
lime juice and red currant jelly. Leave to cool. Whisk the egg
whites stiffly and fold into the apple mixture.

Serving

Sprinkle with the ground cinnamon then pour the honey to cover.
Chill well before serving.

Serves 4

Calories: 84 per portion

Tropical Fruit Mousse

Ingredients

fresh ripe paw paw (1 lb), 4 egg whites
rind and juice of two large limes
4 tablespoons brown sugar

Method

Peel and cut the paw paw into wedges, remove the seeds, then dice into 1 inch cubes. Place the paw paw in a saucepan, add cold water to cover, bring to the boil and simmer for 3 minutes. Pour away the hot water and add ¼ cup of fresh cold water and the sugar. Bring to the boil and allow to simmer until the paw paw is very soft.

Remove from the heat, add the finely grated rind and juice of lime, and liquidise.

Whisk the egg whites stiffly and fold into the puree.

Serving

Pour into individual glasses and chill before serving. Decorate each glass with a pinch of ground ginger.

Serves 4

Calories: 110 per portion

Honey Baked Stuffed Apples

Ingredients

4 large cooking apples
2 oz sultanas, 1 oz butter
4 tablespoons honey

Method

Wash and core the apples with a sharp knife. Score the skin around the middle of each apple. Put a quarter of the sultanas in the centre of each apple and dot each one with a quarter of the butter. Place into an oven-proof dish and pour in enough water to come a quarter way up the apple.

Bake in a hot oven (220°C, Gas Mark 7) for ¾ to 1 hour.

Serving

Pour 1 tablespoon of honey over each apple.

Serves 4

Calories: 145 per portion

Caribbean Currants Sorbet

Ingredients

8 oz black currants
10 oz natural yogurt
3 tablespoons brown sugar, 1 tablespoon gelatine
4 tablespoons water, 2 egg whites
2 tablespoons lime juice

Method

Prepare and cook the black currants until they are very soft.
Liquidise and mix with the yogurt and lime juice in a bowl using a
wooden spoon, over hot water, for about 2 minutes. Stir in the
sugar and the gelatine, (ensure the gelatine dissolves).

Whisk the egg whites stiffly and when the black currant mixture
begins to set, fold in the beaten egg whites.

Serving

Pour into a shallow plastic container and freeze.

Serves 4

Calories: 97 per portion

Paw Paw Sundae

Ingredients

2 medium-sized ripe paw paw
6 tablespoons melba sauce
10 oz natural yogurt
5 wholemeal biscuits

Method

Peel and slice paw paw into wedges. Remove the seeds and arrange in alternating layers with the yogurt, melba sauce and crushed biscuits, in 4 tall glasses. Make sure that you finish each one with a layer of fruit and decorate with whipped double cream.

Serving

Chill before serving.

Serves 4

Calories: 150 per portion

Orange and Coconut Fluff

Ingredients

1 orange jelly, 2 eggs
4 glace cherries, 2 oz brown sugar
2 tablespoons desiccated coconut

Method

Dissolve jelly in a small amount of hot water then make up
$3/4$ pint with cold water.

Separate yolks from whites of eggs, add the sugar to the yolks
then whisk until thick and creamy. Gradually stir the jelly into the
yolk mixture. Leave in a cool place until it begins to set.

Whisk egg whites until fluffy and fold into the almost-set jelly.
Divide the mixture into 4 individual glasses, add a sprinkling of
coconut then crown each with a cherry.

Serving

Serve chilled.

Serves 4

Calories: 225 per portion

CAKES

Sheila Cakes

Brandy Cakes

Classic Coconut Cakes

Coconut Candy Cakes

Ginger Nut Cakes

Grannies Cakes

Sheila Cakes

Ingredients

6 oz self raising flour
4 oz butter, 2 eggs
$\frac{1}{4}$ pint soya milk, 4 oz brown sugar
4 oz currants, a pinch of salt

Method

Sieve the flour and salt into a bowl. Cream the butter and sugar
until light in colour and fluffy in texture. Beat the eggs lightly with
a whisk while gradually adding a small portion of the flour to
make a creamy mixture. Add the milk slowly, then the remaining
flour and the currants, stirring continuously as you go.

Half fill 20 paper cases on a baking sheet and bake on the middle
shelf of a moderately hot oven (190°C, Gas Mark 5) for
20 minutes until a dark golden brown.

Serving

Serve when cool.

Serves 20

Calories: 120 per portion

Brandy Cakes

Ingredients

8 oz wholemeal flour, $\frac{1}{2}$ teaspoon salt
2 eggs, 4 tablespoons vegetable oil, the juice of half a lime
8 oz brown sugar, 3 tablespoons brandy, 1 pint milk

Method

Sieve the flour into a mixing bowl then make a well in the centre and break the eggs into the flour. Add $\frac{1}{4}$ pint of the milk and stir, gradually working in the flour from the sides. Add enough milk to give a stiff batter consistency. Mix thoroughly for at least 5 minutes, then cover and leave to stand for 30 minutes. Add the remaining milk and stir well. Pour the mixture into a jug. Place 1 tablespoon of oil in a small frying pan on medium heat then as the oil begins to smoke, pour in enough batter to cover the bottom of the pan. Tilt the pan to ensure the mixture runs over evenly then increase the heat, while moving the frying pan gently from side to side, and fry until the underside of the cake is brown. Check the sides of the pan to ensure that the cake is free then turn and fry on the other side until brown. Turn out on to a sheet of greaseproof paper.

Serving

Sprinkle with brandy and lime juice before serving.

Serves 8

Calories: 289 per portion

Classic Coconut Cakes

Ingredients

6 oz self raising flour
$\frac{1}{4}$ teaspoon vanilla essence
4 level teaspoons baking powder
2 oz desiccated coconut, 4 tablespoons milk
6 oz brown sugar, 6 oz butter, a pinch of salt, 3 eggs

Method

Grease two 8 inch cake tins and line the bottom of each with a round piece of grease-proof paper. Place the butter, flour, baking powder and salt in a bowl, then add the sugar, eggs, vanilla essence and milk. Mix briskly for 1 minute until evenly mixed, adding another spoonful of milk if necessary to make a dropping consistency. Spoon the mixture into two tins and bake in a moderately hot oven (190°C, Gas mark 5) for 20 minutes, then turn out onto a wire tray to cool.

When at room temperature sandwich together with whipped cream.

Serving

Sprinkle each cake with the coconut flakes before serving.

Serves 12

Calories: 249 per portion

Coconut Candy Cakes

Ingredients

5 oz self raising flour
a pinch of salt
3 oz desiccated coconut
1 egg, 4 oz margarine
4 oz brown sugar

Method

Cream the margarine and sugar in a bowl and mix in the egg. Stir in the flour and coconut then half fill 8 small paper cases with the mixture.

Place on a baking tray and bake in a hot oven (220° C, Gas Mark 7) for about 10 minutes until firm on the top. Cool on wire tray.

Serves 8

Calories: 269 per portion

Ginger Nut Cake

Ingredients

4 oz self raising flour
2 level teaspoons ground ginger
1 level teaspoon cinnamon, 1 tablespoon brown sugar
$\frac{1}{2}$ teaspoon bicarbonate soda, 2 tablespoons vegetable oil
2 tablespoons golden syrup

Method

Place the oil and syrup into a large saucepan over a low heat for about 2 minutes then allow to cool.

Mix and sieve the flour, cinnamon and soda; stir into the saucepan with a wooden spoon until thoroughly mixed. Then, remove small portions of the mixture, the size of a walnut and roll each of these portions into a small ball between the palms of the hand. Place the balls of dough well apart from each other on grease-proof baking paper, on a baking tray. Bake in a moderate oven (190° C, Gas Mark 5) until brown (10 minutes).

Serving

Serve cold.

Serves 15

Calories: 72 per portion

Grannies Cake

Ingredients

8 oz plain flour
2 teaspoons baking powder
4 oz brown sugar, ½ teaspoon mixed spice
4 tablespoons milk, ½ teaspoon salt
4 oz butter, 4 oz mixed fruit
2 eggs

Method

Place the flour, salt, baking powder and mixed spice into a bowl and rub in the butter with tips of fingers until mixture looks like breadcrumbs. Add sugar and mixed fruit. Beat the eggs and stir into the mixture, adding a little milk to mix to a dropping consistency.

Spoon the mix into a 12 inch baking tin and bake in a moderately hot oven (200° C, Gas Mark 6) for 15 minutes until well risen and golden brown. Leave to cool in the tin.

Serving

Serve cold.

Serves 12

Calories: 236 per portion

BREAD AND
BISCUITS

West Indian Shortbread

Gingerbread

White Rum Biscuits

West Indian Shortbread

Ingredients

6 oz plain flour
2 oz cornflour, 4 oz butter
2 oz brown sugar
1 egg yolk

Method

Sieve the flour and cornflour into a bowl then rub in the butter. Add the sugar and stir in the egg yolk, mixing until consistent.

Turn out the mixture onto a floured surface and knead well until smooth and free from cracks. Shape the mixture into a round cake.

Imprint all around the edge with the teeth of a fork.

Bake in a slow oven (160° C, Gas Mark 3) for 45-50 minutes then lift carefully on to a wire tray.

Serving

Sprinkle with brown sugar and leave until cool before serving.

Serves 4

Calories: 480 per portion

Gingerbread

Ingredients

10 oz plain flour, 2 oz cornflour
1 level teaspoon bicarbonate soda, 1 level teaspoon mixed spices
2 level teaspoons ground ginger, 3 oz chopped candied peel
2 oz chopped crystallised ginger, 8 oz treacle
$\frac{1}{4}$ pint soya milk, 6 tablespoons vegetable oil
1 beaten egg, 4 oz soft brown sugar

Method

Sieve flour, corn flour, bicarbonate soda and spices together into a mixing bowl. Stir in the sugar, peel and crystallised ginger. Add the warm treacle, milk, oil and egg and beat well. Pour the mixture immediately into a 2 inch deep baking tin (lightly greased) and bake for $1\frac{1}{4}$ hours in a moderate oven (180°C, Gas Mark 4).

Serving

Serve, when cool, in slices.

Serves 12

Calories: 190 per portion

White Rum Biscuits

Ingredients

8 oz butter
4 oz brown sugar
2 tablespoons Jamaican white rum
12 oz plain flour, 4 oz cornflour

Method

Cream the butter and sugar together very thoroughly. Sieve and mix the flour and cornflour together then gradually work into the creamed butter mixture. Knead the mixture into a round flat shape; place it on a baking tray and crimp the edges between the thumb and forefinger.

Punch a number of holes across the surface of the dough with a fork then bake in a slow oven (160°C, Gas Mark 3), for 30 minutes.

Cut the cake into wedges or fingers and sprinkle with brown sugar.

Serving

Sprinkle with the rum then leave aside for at least 15 minutes before serving.

Serves 12

Calories: 280 per serving

PASTRIES

Flaky Pastry

Suet Pastry

Short Crust Pastry

Flaky Pastry

Ingredients

8 oz flour, 3 oz butter
3 oz lard, cold water to mix
pinch of salt, $^1/_2$ lemon juice

Method

Sieve flour and salt into a bowl. Cream the butter and lard to a soft and pliable mix then divide into four portions. Rub one portion of the fat into the flour, add a squeeze of lemon juice, add sufficient cold water to make a soft dough. Roll the dough into an oblong. Cover 3 inches of this with another portion of the fat, dabbing small pieces over the dough. Fold the dough three times, starting at the bottom with the uncovered section. Bring this up to the centre of the oblong. Bring the top third down over this. Lightly press the edges together with a rolling pin. Turn, then roll it out into an oblong. Repeat this process twice, adding another portion of the fat each time. Fold the pastry (three folds as before), this time without adding fat, then wrap in grease-proof paper and leave in a cool place for an hour before finally rolling out for use.

Serves 4

Calories: 400 per portion.

Note: If possible leave the pastry in a cool place for about 10 minutes before each rolling.

Suet Pastry

Ingredients

8 oz plain flour
1 teaspoon baking powder
a pinch of salt, 4 oz shredded suet
a little water to mix

Method

Sieve flour, baking powder and salt. Add suet and mix in, using a
long wooden spoon. Stir in enough water to make a firm dough.
Knead lightly. Roll out as required.

Serves 4

Calories: 320 per portion

Short Crust Pastry

Ingredients

8 oz plain flour
2 oz lard, 2 oz vegetable margarine
a pinch of salt, cold water to mix

Method

Sieve the flour and salt into a mixing bowl. Roughly chop the fat and add the flour. Rub the fat into the flour using the finger-tips until the mixture resembles breadcrumbs. Gradually add the cold water and knead the mixture lightly by hand until it holds together into a firm dough. Turn out onto a lightly floured surface and knead lightly until smooth. Turn pastry over and roll out as required.

Serves 4

Calories: 290 per portion

Hint: To get the best result from this pastry, keep in the fridge for at least 20 minutes before use.

SAUCES

Caramel Sauce

Coffee Sauce

Lime Sauce

Paw Paw Sauce

Banana Sauce

Spicy Butter Sauce

Caribbean Devilled Sauce

Mango Sauce

Caramel Sauce

Ingredients

4 tablespoons soft brown sugar
4 tablespoons golden syrup, 2 oz butter
4 tablespoons water

Method

Place the sugar and syrup into a saucepan and heat while stirring
until the sugar dissolves. Bring to the boil and simmer for
2 minutes. Allow to cool. Add butter and water. Return to the
heat and boil for a further 2 minutes, then allow to cool.

Serving

This delicious sauce can be served with Bananas Sarah Bernard or
Apple Peekala.

Serves 4

Calories: 180 per portion

Coffee Sauce

Ingredients

$1/2$ pint strong black coffee
3 level tablespoons cornflour, 1 oz butter
2 heaped tablespoons soft brown sugar

Method

Blend the coffee and cornflour together. Place in a small
saucepan. Bring to the boil and simmer on gentle heat for
2 or 3 minutes. Remove from the heat and allow to cool.

Serving

Stir in the sugar and butter before serving. This sauce is ideal with
Brandy Delight or other hot puddings.

Serves 8

Calories: 47 per portion

Lime Sauce

Ingredients

4 tablespoons lime juice
2 pimento berries, 4 tablespoons soya sauce
1 medium sized green pepper
1 medium sized red pepper
a pinch of salt, ground black pepper
1 oz butter, 1 clove garlic chopped
½ pint (hot) water

Method

Peel and chop the garlic very finely. Cut open each pepper and remove the seeds and pith then chop finely. Place the butter in a saucepan and add the chopped garlic and peppers on a low heat, stirring with a wooden spoon. Leave to simmer until the vegetables are cooked, then stir in the pimento berries, soya sauce, ground black pepper, ½ pint hot water, lime juice, salt, ground black pepper and simmer for another 5 minutes.
Remove from the heat and leave aside to cool.
Re-heat when required.

Serving

This spicy lime sauce can be served with any fish dish

Serves 8-10

Calories: 40 per portion

Paw Paw Sauce

Ingredients

1 lb green paw paw
2 oz brown sugar
1 tablespoon lime juice
$^1/_4$ cup hot water (tea cup)

Method

Peel and cut the paw paw into small pieces. Place in a saucepan with tap water to cover and bring to the boil. Pour away the water, drain then add $^1/_4$ cup of hot water and 2 oz sugar, allowing the paw paw to simmer gently on a low heat, until it is very soft. Remove from the heat. Add 1 tablespoon lime juice and liquidise in a blender.

Serving

Serve one or two tablespoons with baked pork or baked ham.

Serves 12

Calories: 45 per portion

Banana Sauce

Ingredients

2 oz firm ripe banana
$^1/_2$ pint soya milk, 2 tablespoons lime juice
2 tablespoons cornflour, 2 tablespoons honey
a pinch of ground nutmeg

Method

Peel and slice the bananas. Place slices in a saucepan with the milk and lime juice. Bring to the boil and simmer for 2 minutes, then mix the cornflour with a little cold water and add the banana mixture while stirring with a wooden spoon. Remove from the heat and stir in the honey and nutmeg. Return to the heat while stirring and simmer for another 3 minutes. Liquidise then leave to cool.

Serving

Serve with ripe bananas or ice cream.

Serves 8

Calories: 70 per portion

Spicy Butter Sauce

Ingredients

$^1/_2$ lb butter (unsalted)
4 pimento (berries), 2 tablespoons lime juice
a pinch of salt, freshly ground black pepper
2 spring onions finely chopped
$^1/_2$ teaspoon curry powder

Method

Place the butter into a bowl and cream the butter with a wooden spoon. Crush the pimento berries and add to the butter mixture along with freshly ground black pepper, garlic (chopped finely), lime juice, salt, onions, curry powder. Mix well until the ingredients are blended into the butter. Place the butter mixture onto a large sheet of foil and freeze until required.

Serving

This sauce can be served with grilled fish or steak. Simply cut slices from frozen block and place directly onto the hot steak or fish.

Serves 12

Calories: 150 per portion

Caribbean Devilled Sauce

Ingredients

1 cup vinegar
2 spring onions, 1 clove garlic
1 tablespoon vegetable oil, $\frac{1}{2}$ teaspoon chilli powder
$\frac{1}{2}$ teaspoon soft brown sugar, 2 large tomatoes chopped finely
4 pimento berries

Method

Peel and chop finely the onions, garlic and tomatoes. Place in a saucepan with the oil and simmer on a gentle heat to allow cooking without colour, for three minutes, stirring with a wooden spoon. Then add chilli powder, brown sugar, vinegar, and crushed pimento berries. Simmer for another minute on a low heat. Remove from the heat and allow to cool.

Serving

This sauce can be served hot or cold.

Serves 16

Calories: 55 per portion

Hint: An ideal sauce for pork dishes.

Mango Sauce

Ingredients

$^1/_2$ pint water
4 medium sized ripe mangoes
1 tablespoon lime juice, 2 tablespoons soft brown sugar
2 tablespoons cornflour, $^1/_2$ teaspoon vanilla essence
$^1/_2$ teaspoon mixed spice

Method

Peel the mangoes and cut off all the flesh from the stone.
Place the mango slices and water into a saucepan, and bring to
the boil. Mix the cornflour with a little cold water and add the
mango slices. Stir well with a wooden spoon on a gentle low heat.
Stir well until the mixture is very smooth, then add lime juice,
sugar, vanilla essence, and mixed spice, stirring always. Simmer
for another 3 minutes. Remove from the heat and leave aside to
cool.

Serving

Serve cold.

Serves 8

Calories: 120 per portion

Note: Delicious with curry dishes, one tablespoon per person is
enough.

Glossary of Terms

Ackee   The fruit of a West African tree introduced to Jamaica by the British. When ripe, the scarlet shell of the ackee splits open to reveal three shiny black seeds surrounded by three segments of edible flesh. The flesh is cooked and served as a vegetable which has a delicate flavour. Fresh ackees are rarely available in Britain but are readily available in tins.

Aubergine   Also known as Eggplant or Belangere, it comes in a variety of sizes and colours, the most common being a deep-purple. It is cooked and eaten as a vegetable.

Avocado   First cultivated in Mexico but now common in most tropical countries. Avocados range from the black wrinkled-skin varieties to the large, green, smooth-skinned types. They are pear-like in shape with a large stone at the centre. The flesh is yellow/green with a buttery texture. Usually sold unripe, they should be kept until the fruit gives a little when gently squeezed. Once cut, the flesh should be sprinkled with lime juice to prevent discolouring.

Banana   A fully ripe banana has no tinges of green and the yellow skin is slightly speckled. Unripe green bananas are cooked and eaten as a starchy vegetable. Boiled with the skin on, both ends of green banana should be clipped and the skin deeply scored with a knife along its length to enable easy removal.

Breadfruit   A large, round, green-skinned fruit cooked as a vegetable. The creamy white flesh has a starchy texture. The central woody core is inedible and should be removed prior to serving.

Callaloo   Originally from Africa, the name refers to the leaves of the taro plant. Pak choy (Chinese spinach) or fresh leaf spinach may be substituted if fresh callaloo is not available.

Cassava   A tropical plant with a long tuberous root covered with bark-like, hairy skin. When peeled, the flesh is white and hard. Cassava is eaten as a vegetable or made into flour for cakes and bread.

Cho cho   Also known as Christophene, the cho cho closely resembles a pear in shape, with a slightly prickly skin, colour ranges from pale green to white. It is boiled and eaten as a vegetable.

Coco   Otherwise known as Eddo or Taro, this is a hairy tuber about the size of a potato. When peeled the flesh is pink or white in colour.

Coconut   Nut of the coconut tree – when buying choose coconuts which are heavy and contain liquid (shake to verify).

Coconut milk   Made by adding the flesh (grated) from one coconut to about 1 pt/550 ml of water. After mixing the liquid is then strained through muslin cloth to extract all the juice. The process may be repeated before the coconut is discarded.

Ginger   A knobbly root with a papery brown skin and moist yellow flesh which has a sharp pungent flavour.

Lime   A citrus fruit, small and round with a bright yellow or green skin. The juice is sharper and has a more distinct flavour than that of the lemon.

Mango   The mango tree is native to Asia but is now widely cultivated in the tropics. The fruits come in different shapes and sizes, the skin ranging in colour when ripe from green to deep red, with flesh tinted yellow to orange. Mangoes have a delicate fragrance and a sweet taste.

Nutmeg   A dark-brown nut added as a spice to both sweet and savoury food. The flavour is far superior when freshly grated.

Okra   Introduced into the Caribbean from Africa, although of tropical Asian origin, it is also known as Ladies' Fingers. The pods are green and tapered and should be eaten young. The principal ingredient in the dish Gumbo. Okra has a rather slimy texture when cooked.

Paw paw   Also called papaya, the long oval fruits are hard and green when unripe. At this stage they are often cooked as a vegetable. When ripe they are yellow/orange in colour and slightly soft. The flesh inside is yellow or coral-coloured and the centre filled with small black seeds.

Peanut milk   To make peanut milk, remove shell and inner skin of the peanuts and blend 4 oz/115 g (unshelled weight) with 1/2 pt/275 ml water. Strain through muslin and sweeten with honey.

Pepper   Both the sweet bell-peppers or capsicums, and the hot peppers originated from Mexico. The hot peppers of the Caribbean, sometimes called Scotch Bonnet peppers because of their wrinkled appearance, may be pale green, yellow, orange, or red. The seeds are best removed to reduce the fiery taste.

Pimento   Also known as Allspice or Jamaican Pepper, it is the dried berry of a tree native to Jamaica. Closely resembling peppercorns, the pimento has the combined flavour of nutmeg, cinnamon and cloves.

Pineapple   Perhaps the most popular tropical fruit. When ripe, it should give slightly when pressed.

Plantain   A member of the banana family, the plantain is only eaten cooked, ripe or unripe. When green, the thick skin of the plantain is difficult to remove.

Sweet potato   Round or elongated tubers native to South America. The skin is reddish brown, pink or white, the flesh ranges from yellow to white and is slightly sweet.

Yam   There are several varieties of this edible tuber (Yellow yam, Negro yam, etc.) and the size and shape vary enormously. When peeled of its thick tough skin, the flesh is yellow or white (occasionally purple) with a nut-like flavour. It is boiled and eaten as a vegetable.

Index

T

tomato 23, 24
treacle 123

V

vanilla 17, 104
vegetable oil 22, 25, 26
vegetables
    ackee 30, 33, 76
    banana 31, 52, 62
    breadfruit 33
    cabbage 63
    callaloo 31, 34, 65
    cho cho 30, 34, 52, 65, 75, 91
    coco 71
    pumpkin 32, 34, 52
    sweet potato 34, 77
    sweetcorn 32, 34, 62
    yam 34, 62, 65, 68

W

watercress 80
wholemeal flour 22, 25, 26, 115

Y

yam 72, 82
yogurt 23, 94, 102, 105, 110